<The Power of CODING/>

The Power of PHP

Grace Murphy

Cavendish Square
New York

Published in 2018 by Cavendish Square Publishing, LLC
243 5th Avenue, Suite 136, New York, NY 10016

First Edition

Library of Congress Cataloging-in-Publication Data

Names: Murphy, Grace.
Title: The power of PHP / Grace Murphy.
Description: New York : Cavendish Square Publishing, 2018. | Series: The power of coding | Includes bibliographical references and index.
Identifiers: ISBN 9781502629463 (library bound) | ISBN 9781502634191 (pbk.) | ISBN 9781502629470 (ebook)
Subjects: LCSH: Computer programming--Juvenile literature. | PHP (Computer program language).
Classification: LCC QA76.73.P224 M87 2018 | DDC 006.7--dc23

Editorial Director: David McNamara
Editor: Caitlyn Miller
Copy Editor: Rebecca Rohan
Associate Art Director: Amy Greenan
Designer: Joe Parenteau
Production Coordinator: Karol Szymczuk
Photo Research: J8 Media

The photographs in this book are used by permission and through the courtesy of: Front cover, Hero Images/Alamy Stock Photos; p. 4 Vincent Pontier/http://www.elroubio.net/elephpant_download.php http://php.net/elephpant.php/File: Webysther 20160423 - Elephpant.svg/Wikimedia Commons; p. 6 William Stadtwald Demchick, own work/File: Rasmus Lerdorf August 2014 (cropped).jpg/Wikimedia Commons; p.13 BestVectorIcon/Shutterstock.com; p. 19 (right) Ben Scholzen (https://www.flickr.com/people/30771817@N06) from Karlsruhe, Deutschland/Andi Gutmans holding the keynote (https://www.flickr.com/photos/dasprid/5141279580/)/File: Andi Gutmans holding the keynote (5141279580).jpg/Wikimedia Commons, (left) Léo Lefebvre, own work/File: ZeevSuraski2.jpg/Wikimedia Commons; p. 28 Magictorch/Ikon Images/Getty Images; p. 34 Defense Advanced Research Projects Agency (DARPA)/File: DARPA Big Data.jpg/Wikimedia Commons; p. 40 Georgejmclittle/Shutterstock.com; p. 45 WizardCat (http://wizardcat.com/)/published (https://cms-assets.tutsplus.com/legacy-premium-tutorials/posts/52639/images/52639_d94d3f3cd9aa454a8e0bf3b1932536cd.png) on tuts+ (http://code.tutsplus.com/tutorials/why-laravel-is-taking-the-php-community-by-storm--pre-52639)/File: Logo-composer-tutsplus.png/Wikimedia Commons; p. 50 Alex Mit/Shutterstock.com; p. 53 Larry Ewing (http://www.isc.tamu.edu/~lewing/linux/), gg3po (http://kde-look.org/usermanager/search.php?username=gg3po)/lewing@isc.tamu.edu (mailto:lewing@isc.tamu.edu), The GIMP (http://isc.tamu.edu/~lewing/linux//File: NewTux.svg/Wikimedia Commons; p. 54 Jeff Sandquist (http://www.flickr.com/people/48003527@N00)/File: MIX Keynote-Scott Guthrie 09 MS 05 2007.jpg/Wikimedia Commons; p. 61 MaxKobuzan/Shutterstock.com; p. 67 FGRibreau, own work/File: Redsmin-Redis-gui.png/Wikimedia Commons; JovanCormac, own work/File: MySQLQueryBrowser.jpg/Wikimedia Commons; p. 70 Tonusamuel, own work/File: 20170531-DSC06942.jpg/Wikimedia Commons; p. 72 Africa Studio/Shutterstock.com; p. 78 Monkey Business Images/Shutterstock.com; p. 79 Rawpixel Ltd/Alamy Stock Photo; p. 82 karmatosed (https://www.flickr.com/people/73631307@N00) from UK/File: Matt Mullenweg (31537986015).jpg/Wikimedia Commons; p. 83 Christian Rummel/iStock Unreleased/Getty Images; p. 86 Milesjpool, own work/File: CPT-Object-Var-Proc.svg/Wikimedia Commons; p. 89 Enrique Dans (http://www.flickr.com/people/16189770@N00) from Madrid, Spain/File: Tim Berners-Lee April 2009.jpg/Wikimedia Commons; p. 95 Dean Drobot/Shutterstock.com; p. 98 Wilgengebroed on Flickr (https://www.flickr.com/photos/wilgengebroed/)/File: Internet of things signed by the author.jpg/Wikimedia Commons.

Printed in the United States of America

<Contents/>

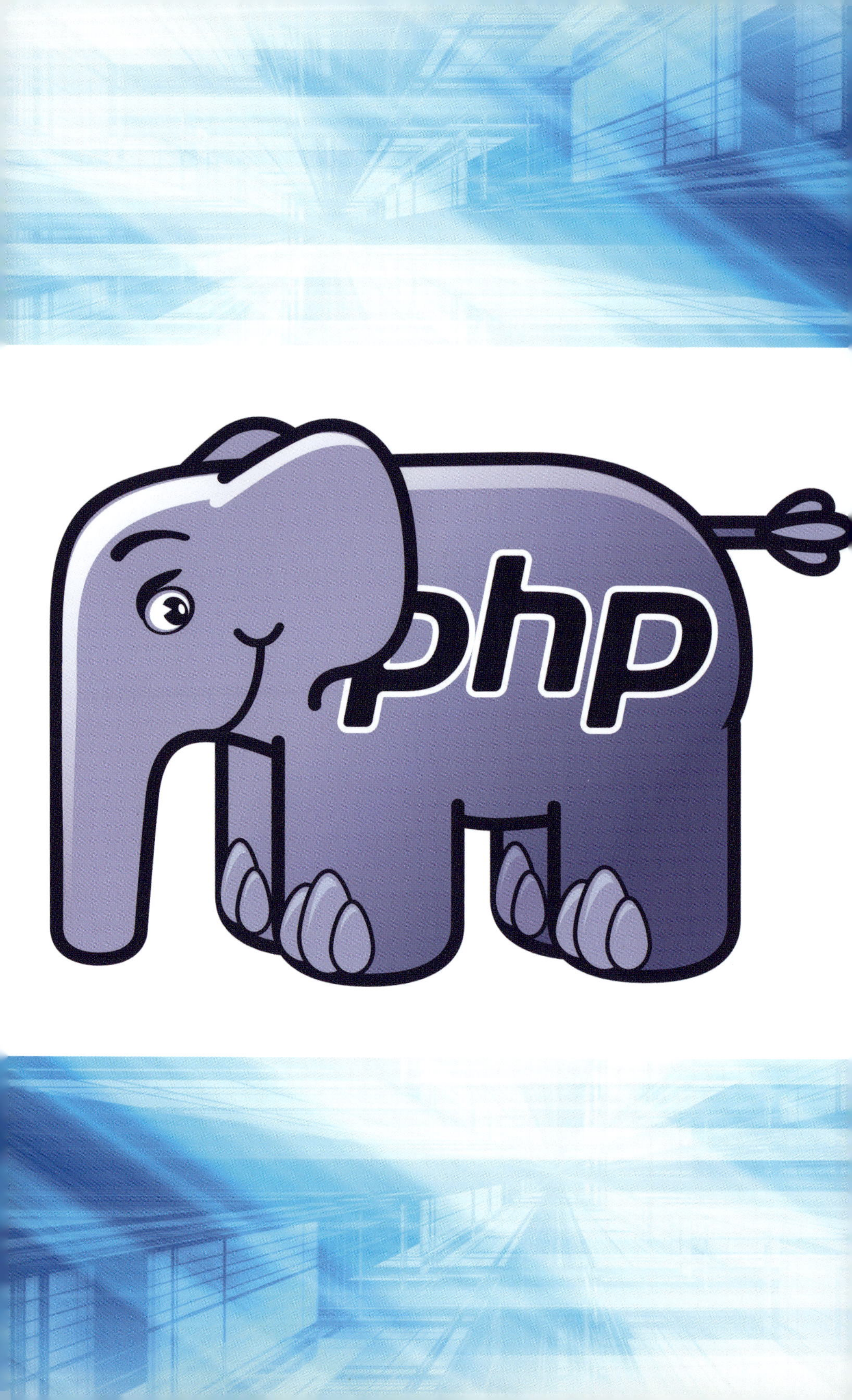
php

<Chapter One/>

The History of PHP

Every time you log on to Facebook, check Wikipedia for information you are curious about, or connect to a WordPress-created web page, **applications** written using PHP make it possible. PHP is what is known as a server-side **scripting language**, meaning it's written to automate certain tasks and run on the **server** rather than on the user's own computer. This immensely popular programming language helps accomplish tasks as varied as creating secure logins, accessing a multitude of databases, and incorporating Flash videos in dynamic web pages (web pages featuring

Opposite: PHP's mascot is the ElePHPant.

content that changes based on user interaction). Some estimates indicate that PHP supports one-third of the web. Despite the complex web pages it is used to create, PHP is easy for novice programmers to learn. It also has many advanced features for more experienced programmers. But beyond PHP's huge potential for programmers of all skill levels, it also has a fascinating history.

The Origins of PHP

As Rasmus Lerdorf, the originator of PHP tells it, he was not interested in creating a programming language, he just wanted to solve a problem. The Danish-Canadian systems engineer was looking for an easy way to develop and maintain his personal web page. So in 1994, he began working on the original PHP component, which was a **common gateway interface (CGI)**. Lerdorf used the general-purpose programming language C to establish the components that would help him maintain his personal home page. Thus, he called his creation PHP Tools after "personal home page" and released it to the public.

Rasmus Lerdorf created PHP.

This first version, also called PHP 1, can still be downloaded at www.museum.php.net.

Lerdorf had decided to make his software **open-source**. This meant that his solution would be freely and publicly accessible. It could also be shared and modified. According to Lerdorf, people participate in open-source software development for several reasons, including self-interest (Lerdorf's self-identified motivation), because they have a problem they want solved; self-expression, because it satisfies their creative impulse; and altruism, because they want to improve the world.

The open-source movement had begun in the United States in the 1950s with academics sharing software among their colleagues. Soon, though, computer hardware manufacturers began charging for the software that was used on their machines. By the 1980s, some technology leaders were dissatisfied with the steadily rising software costs. They formed the GNU project to develop a software operating system that **developers** and users would be free to use, distribute, modify, and improve. The Linux operating system, with millions of users today, was the first result of that project.

Although the term "open-source" was not coined until 1998, by the mid-1990s, when Lerdorf began developing his web scripting tools, the movement was gaining traction with the growth of dotcom companies.

Rasmus Lerdorf

○ ○ ○

"As strange as it may sound, I don't actually like programming. My passion is for developing systems that simplify complicated problems."—Rasmus Lerdorf

Rasmus Lerdorf, original creator of PHP, was born on Disko Island, off the coast of Greenland in Baffin Bay, on November 22, 1968. His early years were spent in Denmark. In 1980, he moved with his family to Canada. They settled in King City, Ontario, in 1983. Lerdorf attended King City Secondary School, where he played soccer and basketball.

He began developing his computer skills as a teenager by writing software for the Unisys ICON, a system built specifically for Ontario's schools. These computers, according to Lerdorf, didn't have much software and "nobody knew anything about them." With his friend Ben Eng, Lerdorf created software for this distinctive machine and ended up teaching an adult education computer course. He also taught an accreditation program for teachers. Lerdorf credits these early experiences with providing both a stimulus and a solid base for his later interests.

Lerdorf enrolled at the University of Waterloo, whose Cheriton School of Computer Science produced roughly one-third of Canada's computer science graduates in the 1980s. At that time, any student who could demonstrate the ability to crash the computer system was treated to a drink for uncovering a weakness. Lerdorf was part of the computer co-op program and worked in several Canadian locations. In his final assignment, he worked with Nutec, a software company in Brazil. With his experiences in a variety of countries, Lerdorf became fluent in five spoken languages, as well as multiple computer languages. He graduated in 1993 with a Bachelor of Applied Science in Systems Design Engineering.

He continued with Nutec after graduation and was transferred to Silicon Valley shortly thereafter. Lerdorf became very excited about working with the web, which was then an up-and-coming technology field. Dissatisfied with his company's commitment to web projects, Lerdorf moved back to Toronto and began working as a consultant. In Toronto, he developed the initial version of PHP, a web scripting language, and worked on the Apache web server, which was then emerging as the most generally used web-server software.

His consultant work included a large project with the University of Toronto that facilitated online access for students and faculty, followed by work with Bell Global Solutions. After a brief sojourn in North Carolina with IBM's WebSphere team, Lerdorf moved back to Silicon Valley, attracted by the dotcom explosion. He participated in an unsuccessful startup while continuing to work on new versions of PHP. By this time, although Lerdorf never intended PHP to be a full-fledged programming language, his original web scripting solutions had expanded exponentially and organically into a popular web language with hundreds of contributors working on this open-source project.

Lerdorf was hired in 2002 to help the search engine site Yahoo!. At the time, Yahoo! was the most popular web destination, and Lerdorf helped them make PHP work more effectively. In 2003, the MIT Technology Review named him as one of the top 100 innovators in the world under the age of thirty-five. He stayed with Yahoo! until 2009. He subsequently worked for three more sites, WePay, Etsy, and Jelastic, and consulted for startups. Today, Lerdorf travels around the world to speak at open-source seminars and conferences. Despite his avowed dislike for programming, Lerdorf is acknowledged as the creator of one of the most widely used web development languages.

In particular, the Apache **HTTP** server, which played a critical role in the development of the World Wide Web and is today the most used web software in the world, was released as open-source software.

PHP soon was adopted by the open-source community, allowing developers to improve upon the code and fix any bugs. Lerdorf extended the initial components to have a much wider capacity that included **web forms** and the ability to transmit and receive information from databases. He called this version PHP/FI (for forms **interpreter**) and, but only briefly, dropped the PHP designation and identified his scripting tools simply as FI.

This early version of PHP included some of the basic functions that still exist in PHP today. It could automatically interpret form variables and had a limited ability to embed **HTML** (hypertext markup language) **syntax**. Since HTML is the most basic building block of the web, both describing and defining the content of a web page, this capacity was critical. FI continued to receive greater acceptance, but it was not yet considered to be a full-fledged programming language.

By April 1996, Lerdorf had completed another revision and again called the new product PHP/FI. In this second generation, PHP was evolving into a real programming language, rather than just a set of tools. It had a similar structure to C, which made it easier for C developers to use it. Its ability to function on a greater variety of operating systems was being explored. This version also supported **cookies** and user-defined functions, as well as MySQL, an open-source database management system. In June, the name of PHP/FI was changed to PHP 2.0. After a short period of being called Personal Home Page Construction Kit, it had been accepted as the next generation of PHP.

PHP 2.0 had a very short shelf life after it was officially released in November 1997. Despite its limitations, though, it was becoming very popular with web developers. According to a survey in May 1998, nearly sixty thousand domains (at that time approximately 1 percent of all domains) used servers that had PHP installed. PHP 2.0 did not have many contributors, however, and was essentially written by Lerdorf alone. Even at the time the 2.0 version was released, it was already being rewritten by the open-source community.

PHP 3

In 1997, Andi Gutmans and Zeev Suraski, students at the Technion in Tel Aviv, Israel, began working on an e-commerce application for a university project. They were using PHP but found it was not as efficient as they wanted it to be, and it did not contain a variety of features that they needed. Working in conjunction with Lerdorf, they began a comprehensive rewrite of the PHP **parser**.

Since parsers take source code and translate it into a data structure that can, after **interpretation**, be used to execute programs, an effective parser is a powerful computer-language component at the core of the language itself. This new makeover, with the collaboration of Gutmans, Suraski and Lerdorf, was designed to incorporate many improvements and build upon the PHP 2.0 user base. The newer version actually closely resembled the PHP language as it is used today. It was named PHP 3.0. This new version also had a renamed acronym to better reflect its many uses: the full meaning of PHP now became—rather than Personal Home Page—PHP: Hypertext Preprocessor.

The open-source PHP 3 attracted a number of new developers as well as many new users. The language was easy to extend, and many developers added a variety of **modules** to increase its usefulness. These included interfaces with multiple databases, connections to new **protocols**, and **Application Program Interfaces (API)**. PHP 3 also included support for **object-oriented programming (OOP)**, a model that is organized around objects and data, rather than action steps and logic. This type of program

Developers added a variety of modules to PHP 3, including support for Application Program Interfaces (APIs).

makes it easier to use code written for one program in another and to modify programs over time.

All these features increased the appeal of PHP 3. The announcement making PHP 3 the official successor to PHP/FI was made by the new PHP Development Team in June 1998, after nine months of public testing. By that time, it was already installed on more than seventy thousand domains. It was also hosted on servers using Windows and Macintosh operating systems, as well as the original **Unix** and the operating systems modeled on that system, like Linux. At its height, PHP 3 could be found on approximately 10 percent of internet servers worldwide.

Books on PHP were beginning to make an appearance. The first was a book in Czech by Jirka Kosek called *Creating Interactive Internet Applications*. Shortly thereafter a book in Dutch by Egon Schmid, Christian Cartus, and Richard Blume, entitled *PHP*, was published. *Core PHP Programming* by Leon Atkinson, the first PHP book in English, followed shortly afterward. These early publications preceded a large number of PHP books that were written in different languages and published all over the world. There are over four hundred PHP books in English, over one hundred in German, and more than fifty books in Spanish or French. Other languages include Japanese, Hebrew, and Korean. The scope of PHP publications is another indication of the enormous success of the language.

The ElePHPant in the Room

In 1998, the mascot for PHP was designed. A man named Vincent Pontier created the adorable image now associated with the PHP language and community when he was visited at home by a computer-programming friend who described for him the revolutionary contribution of PHP. While Pontier's friend told him about the ways in which this language would completely change the interactions on the web, Pontier was distractedly doodling the letters PHP on a white piece of paper.

As Pontier tells it: "By chance—chance sometimes [does] make good things happen—I suddenly noticed that the letters were forming the shape of an elephant if viewed in a 'sideways angle.'" Pontier sent his design to Jean-Pierre Dezelus, the owner of a personal website that would eventually transform into PHPinfo.net, a site for PHP resources. Unknown to Pontier, Dezelus was a collector of elephant paraphernalia, and he asked Pontier to create a true elephant logo. Pontier thought that naming it "elePHPant" was a good pun.

The expanding PHP community soon adopted the elePHPant, and it is now known around the world. Later, the logo would also be transformed into a stuffed animal, ever-present at PHP seminars and conferences. The PHP elePHPant has had many incarnations. Although the original elePHPant was blue, a purple elePHPant was created for a PHP Women's Kickstarter campaign, a black one was used for an AmsterdamPHP user group Kickstarter drive, and other elePHPants have been made in orange, red, and aqua for a variety of specialty purposes. There is even a wooly mammoth PHP plush animal, said to be the ancient ancestor of

expanded even more and, in 2001, Netcraft's Web Server Survey indicated that there were 1.8 million sites using PHP.

There were, however, some concerns that PHP releases were not adequately tested for use. A PHP Quality Assurance Initiative was created, shortly after the release of PHP 4 in 2000 to address these criticisms. The first PHP conference was held in Germany in October of the same year. At the O'Reilly Open Source Convention, held in San Diego in 2001, an official PHP conference was included. Now PHP conferences are regularly held at locations around the globe.

Zend and the PHP License

When Gutmans and Suraski founded Zend Technologies to provide business support for the use of PHP in 1998, they also created a new PHP license. The license specifies that "products derived from this software may not be called 'PHP,' nor may 'PHP' appear in their name, without prior written permission from group@php.net. You may indicate that your software works in conjunction with PHP by saying '*Foo* for PHP' instead of calling it 'PHP Foo' or 'phpfoo.'"

Providing services for open-source (and therefore free) software is one business model that allows developers to make money from their involvement in

Zeev Suraski (*left*) and Andi Gutmans (*right*) are the founders of Zend Technologies.

open-source projects. Public domain software, which is not copyrighted, may be free, but anyone can make a modified **proprietary** version and charge for it. Some free programs may actually be copyrighted but are distributed under licenses that allow ownership of a version that has been modified.

Zend uses a model in which the open-source community develops the primary program (in this

Zend Technologies, the PHP Company

○ ○ ○

Andi Gutmans and Zeev Suraski worked in collaboration with Rasmus Lerdorf, the original creator of PHP, to create PHP 3.0. In 1998, Gutmans and Suraski completely reworked and redesigned the PHP core in order to improve the language's basic code and its performance of complex operations. The redesigned parser was named the Zend Engine, and the next release of PHP, PHP 4.0, was based on the Zend Engine. It increased the program's efficiency and supported, among other improvements, improved security for user input.

The following year, Gutmans and Suraski founded Zend Technologies to provide business applications for PHP. Gutmans played several critical roles at Zend. He secured initial funding investments for the startup company including Israeli venture capital funds Platinum Neurone Ventures and Walden Israel; he headed the Advanced Technology Group, focused on strategy and innovation; and he engineered several strategic alliances, including some with business titans like Oracle, IBM, and Microsoft. In 2004, Zend moved its headquarters to Cupertino, California, where it continued to garner millions in investment funding. The Israeli Venture Association gave Zend the Best Startup Software Company award in 2006.

Calling itself the "PHP company," Zend continued to develop software that now includes a variety of products for web applications based on the PHP language. Its software allows programmers to create applications in PHP that accomplish tasks as varied as the protection of intellectual property and the ability to provide online training. Its Zend Server runs and manages web PHP applications. The Zend Platform checks PHP applications for performance problems. In addition to software development, Zend created a system for PHP certification and, by 2013, over ten thousand programmers had received this credential.

Gutmans was named Zend CEO in February 2009, and Zend continued to expand its offerings and its business. In October 2015, Zend was acquired by Rogue Wave, a Colorado software company that supports quick development of enterprise software applications (applications built for companies). According to Suraski, now Chief Technical Officer at Zend, the partnership with Rogue Wave "is a continuation of our vision to support the PHP community and make PHP use easy, accessible, and secure in demanding environments."

case PHP itself), and Zend makes development tools for web applications that are written in PHP. Zend maintains a significant involvement in the continuing improvement and revision of the basic programs, but it does not have specific control over the process. By focusing on the needs of the business community, Zend was first able to get investors and eventually grow into an organization with high earnings.

PHP 5

The next version of PHP took several years of development and a number of pre-releases that came out before the final, official release. But in July 2004, PHP 5.0 was distributed. This new version was powered by Zend Engine 2.0 and used a newly integrated object-oriented programming model as well as the traditional logic model. It added significant capabilities and performance improvements. It supported **eXtensible markup language (XML)**, which is designed to communicate data, unlike HTML, which is designed to display that data. It included built-in Simple Object Access Protocol (SOAP) extensions that permitted users to call on web services and get responses independent of their operating system or the programming language they used.

In the next few years, PHP 5 underwent several revisions. PHP 5.1, released in 2005, continued to add performance enhancements. It simplified database handling and provided better time zone support. It also added more than thirty new functions with various extensions. PHP 5.2, released in 2006, added even more performance improvements. It included a new memory manager, incorporated in the Zend Engine. PHP 5.2 added many new features and provided fixes for more than 200 bugs. PHP 5.3 introduced many new upgrades, particularly using a better object model useful for complex applications. It also fixed more than 140 bugs.

The PHP development team expanded to include new participants, both individuals and organizations. In addition to programmers working directly on PHP code, many others worked on supporting or related projects, such as PHP documentation and PECL, the PHP Extension Community Library. The team relied on a network infrastructure of more than one hundred web servers on six continents. By 2008, PHP 5 was the only stable version under development and the transition from PHP 4 to PHP 5, promoted by the GoPHP5 initiative, was effectively implemented.

Commercial uses of PHP continued to expand with PHP 5. Oracle declared PHP "ready for enterprise use." Yahoo! standardized its operations on PHP. Zend Technologies formed strategic partnerships with IBM and Microsoft. And Zend CTO Zeev Suraski said that PHP "was no longer considered a nice toy and a nice language for simple stuff. It was evident that we could support one of the largest internet sites in the world."

The Version That Wasn't

While PHP 5 was enjoying immense popularity, it was also being criticized because it did not include core language support for Unicode, an industry standard for encoding, representing, and handling text in most of the written languages on the globe. Because of Unicode's widespread use in computer software, Andrei Zmievski led a project in 2005 to bring Unicode support to PHP.

The inclusion of Unicode components to PHP would require a major revision of the language, both in its core software and its user code. The plan for PHP 6 was to release it as the new PHP version with both the Unicode changes as well as other added features then being developed. This plan ran into major roadblocks.

Zmievski's effort was plagued by a shortage of programmers who actually understood the intricacies of the necessary changes and by ongoing performance problems that seemed unable to be resolved. The project was delayed and, instead, PHP 5.3 was released in 2009, incorporating many of the features planned for PHP 6, including a built-in web server that could be used for testing (but without Unicode support). The project in its original form was abandoned in 2010, with the hope that a future revision would include the integration of Unicode. That hope has not yet been realized.

PHP Moves On

Beginning on June 28, 2011, the PHP Group, which is made up of major PHP developers including Lerdorf, Gutmans, Suraski and Zmievski, as well as other significant contributors, decided on a timeline for the release of new versions of PHP. Other minor but official revisions of PHP were then issued: PHP 5.4, PHP 5.5, and PHP 5.6.

PHP continued to build its business base and its web presence. PHP software development kits using cloud-based features were provided by Amazon Web Services and Windows Azure. Facebook developed the HipHop Virtual Machine (HHVM) to convert PHP code into a code compiled dynamically at runtime, improving performance significantly. WordPress, using PHP as its scripting language, had become the number-one blogging site and was emerging as the preeminent web page creation tool. By 2017, it was used by 27 percent of the top ten million websites. In 2013, Google announced that PHP was now a language being supported in AppEngine, their cloud-hosting platform. Google explained that PHP support had become the most requested feature, running on 75 percent of the web sites on the platform.

In 2014, PHP developed its own formal language specification. The PHP Group worked to set standards for the PHP **semantics** and syntax (semantics is the meaning assigned to the characters, words, and symbols used in PHP; the syntax is the structure of the PHP code). Up until this time, PHP functioned with only user documentation. As more applications began to use PHP, it had become more important to establish these standards.

The Next Generation: PHP 7

The naming of the next major PHP revision was a subject of debate. Even though PHP 6 had never been released, the developers felt that giving the number 6 to the new version might cause some confusion. So, after more than two years in development, when the new generation of PHP was announced, it was called PHP 7.

As a result of the continuing desire to improve the performance of PHP, a branch of the language called phpng (PHP next generation) was developed by programmers named Dmitry Stogov, Xinchen Hui, and Nikita Popov. It supported just-in-time **(JIT) compilation**, which improves performance times. The performance enhancement of phpng was recognized and phpng was merged into the master language. In fact, it became the basis of PHP 7. The Zend Engine was redesigned to accommodate the significant changes resulting from phpng, and the new software was called Zend Engine 3.

In December 2016, one year after it was announced, the official version of PHP 7 was released. Some of the features incorporated in PHP 7 included performance at least twice as fast as PHP 5.6. As an example, before phpng, the WordPress homepage required approximately 9.4 billion central processing unit (**CPU**) instructions to execute. With PHP 7, it requires 72 percent fewer instructions—approximately 2.6 billion. The new version also incorporated a secure random number generator, an enormous reduction in memory usage, and the removal of old, unsupported extensions. PHP 7 also introduced new **operators**, such as the "space ship" operator (⇔), useful in comparisons and sorting.

PHP 7 demonstrated the tremendous development of PHP from a limited set of tools created for Rasmus Lerdorf's home page into a sophisticated language that powers websites like WordPress and Wikipedia. In fact, it is now ranked as the third most-used language on the web, after Java and Python.

<Chapter Two/>

How PHP Works

PHP is what is known as a server-side scripting language. This means that it runs on an internet web server, a computer at a remote location that will process web requests and send web pages back to the user, rather than processing them on the user's own computer. So, in order to appreciate how PHP functions, it is important to have some basic knowledge of how the internet itself works.

Opposite: The internet connects the world. Programming languages like PHP make it possible.

A Closer Look at the Internet

All over the world, computers and computer networks are linked through the global network known as the internet. This network is connected in a variety of ways, including telephone wires, fiber optic land lines, satellites, microwave links, and cables laid under the ocean. Despite all the different ways in which the parts of this vast network are connected, it handles all data in the same way. Within this uniformity of data transfer though, the internet can pass on many different types of data, including emails, web pages, and messages, from one computer to another and one network to another. One familiar form of data exchange that provides document storage and access, usually in the form of web pages, happens on what is known as the World Wide Web, a system of servers on the internet. One of the major uses of PHP is the creation of many of those web pages.

Web pages themselves are documents that have been specially formatted in what is called a mark-up language, the most common being HTML. Markup languages provide extra information about the visual appearance of text in a document, including how it should be formatted for display or printing. When a user types in a web address, or URL (Uniform Resource Locator), usually in the form www.webaddress.suffix, the user is connected to the web server at that location.

The web page located at that address on the server computer is transferred to the user's computer, and the document, formatted using HTML, can be viewed by the user. Most documents use HTML or similar markup languages. However, when a document is transmitted using *only* HTML, it does not contain most of the features now expected—such as interactivity and audio and graphics. Something more has to happen with a web page so that users are connected and engaged in a variety of ways and not just reading the content. Rather than the static (unchanging) web pages created with only HTML, web designers create dynamic web pages with content that can change based on the interests or responses of the user. These dynamic web pages are generated in real-time through the use of scripting languages. The essential feature of a scripting language is its ability to manage the activities of other programs, telling them what to do, in the same way that a play script indicates what an actor should do to play a part.

Dynamic Scripting

There are two ways a website can be made dynamic. In order to create dynamic web pages, web applications may contain code that is processed on the user's browser (the user's browser is known as the client), or on the web server.

PHP—Is It a Language?

The 1s and 0s of binary code are the simplest form of computer coding. PHP is far more complex, though it took time before it was recognized as a language.

When Rasmus Lerdorf first developed PHP, it was not thought of as a programming language. It was simply code written to help Lerdorf create a dynamic web page. However, what was useful to Lerdorf turned out to be useful to other programmers, and PHP's popularity grew.

Many programming languages, like Java and C, were developed through specific projects intended to create those languages. Even Ruby, the object-oriented scripting language originally developed for a Japanese market, was thought of as a new programming language from the beginning. Lerdorf himself, though, called his efforts a "tool box," not a language. He said, "There was never any intent to write a programming language … I have absolutely no idea how to write a programming language, I just kept adding the next logical step on the way."

However, the energy and direction of the open-source community led to the adoption of PHP as a widespread and well-liked method for creating dynamic web pages—whether it was called a language or not. Although some claimed it couldn't be a "real" language because it was not consistent and it was not compiled, others claimed that it met the minimum requirements for being considered a language: using syntactical constructs, it instructed the computer to perform certain operations.

PHP also lacked any strong design principles or solid theoretical principles and was thought of, even by those who considered it to be a language, as messy and lacking rigor. Its implementation was dependent upon user documentation. Although that documentation was extensive, its extensiveness led to problems. Furthermore, some basic features, like correct handling of foreign language and Unicode characters, were add-ons that were not cleanly integrated.

As previously mentioned, in 2014, PHP finally got a complete definition of its semantics and its syntax in a document called a draft specification. The draft specification was intended to "evolve over time with the help of everyone who cares about the PHP language," just like other open-source products do. But, although it would be a document that would continue to change and mature, it provided, for the first time, a structure for the future development of PHP. However PHP was initially created, and however it had evolved, after twenty undefined years PHP had finally become a full-fledged computer programming language.

Many major business organizations use this database.

- DB2: This database was created in 1983, although its development began in the 1970s. It was originally used extensively in conjunction with mainframe systems. DB2 is now being used in many large-scale Enterprise Resource Planning (ERP) and e-commerce systems.
- PostgreSQL: Compared to MySQL, PostgreSQL has many advanced features that compare well with the advanced features in Oracle. It is, however, believed to be a bit slower than MySQL.
- Sybase: This database solution is a popular choice for enterprise database management, and it can operate well when a large database is needed.

Although these are the most frequently implemented databases with PHP applications, PHP can support a wide variety of less popular databases, from Mongo to Tokyo Tyrant.

A server-side script, then, creates the communication link between a user, the web server, and the databases. It requests, edits, adds to, and deletes items in the database. In providing this link, the server-side script has many functions:

- It collects data from forms.
- It processes any user input, such as username and password, and it interacts with databases.
- It queries the databases in order to accomplish tasks like password validation.
- It updates the database.
- It sends and receives cookies.
- It encodes the generated web page into HTML.
- It transfers the requested web pages for display on the client browser.
- It encrypts data for security.

Some examples will help illustrate how this server-side scripting works.

Example One: Placing an Order

E-commerce sites are frequently written using server-side scripting. Let's imagine that a customer wants to purchase replacement toner for a laser printer. She enters a Google search for companies that sell laser toners, and the request is transmitted to the Google web server, via HTTP. The web server uses a scripting application that resides on the server, in order to process this request. The application sends a query to the Google database, looking for matches. When a

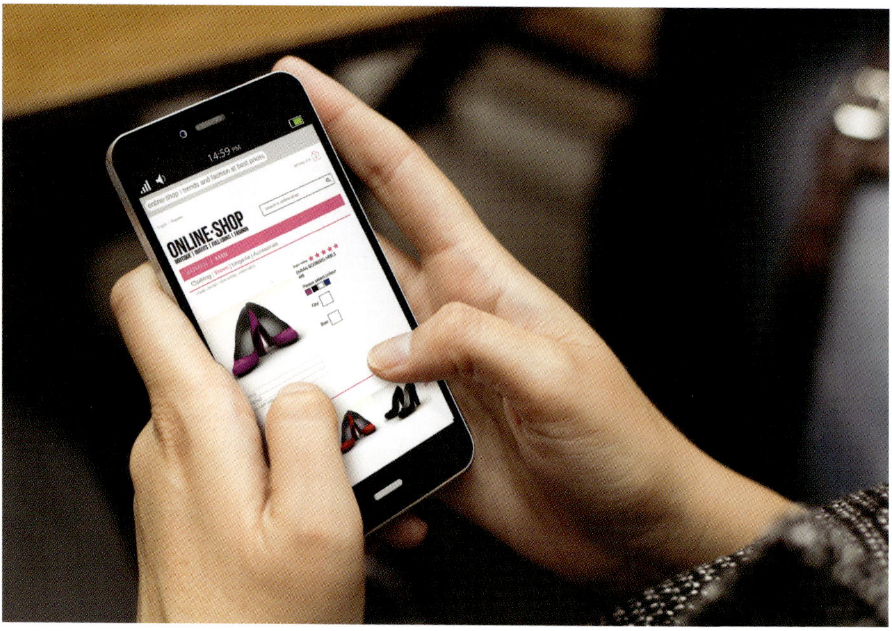

Online shopping is a great example of server-side scripting at work.

match is found, the application generates a web page in HTML that contains the matches found on the database. Often, this web page is created simply by inserting the matching data in an HTML template, and the process is simplified and speedy. Now the newly created web page, responding to the customer's inquiry and providing a list of toner sales companies, is transmitted back to the customer's client browser, again using the HTTP protocols.

The customer next selects the website she wants to use from the list of companies on the web page that is now displayed on her browser. She clicks on the link, which connects to the chosen company's web server. The company's web page, which uses a scripting application written in PHP, is transferred from the company's server to the user's browser. This web page contains a number of input forms for the user to complete. She is asked to identify her printer make and model and the color(s) of toner she needs. When she has filled in the forms, she clicks on the submit button on the web page. Now the information is transferred back to the company's web server. There, the scripting application connects to the database that contains information about printers, matches with the correct toners, and lists the price of each toner by color. The scripting application, once again, creates a web page "on the fly," containing the information extracted from the toner database. This new web page is transmitted back to the user's browser.

This page contains the information about the available toners and also has a form for the customer to complete if she wants to place an order. Filling in the form that requests that an order be placed and clicking to submit it once again transmits this information back to the company web server. The scripting application processes this request and sends a page back to the client for the customer to fill out with billing and shipping information. When the company web server receives this new information, the scripting application matches it to a database of customers that is also on the company's server. If she is a new customer, the information will be added to the company's customer database. If the information is a partial match, a web page that requests more information, for example an updated shipping address, will be generated. If the customer responds with new information, the database will be edited to include it. When the information has been verified, the customer will be requested to review the order details on a web page that was generated at the server with all the current data. If the customer accepts this information and completes the transaction, the database will be updated and the order will be placed.

Example Two: Connecting to Social Media

Server-side scripts provide the interactivity on social media sites. Facebook, for example, uses PHP as its basic programming language. So, if a user wants to edit the information that is on his profile, he will first log in to his Facebook account with his username and password. This login information will be transferred to the Facebook server (actually one of the over sixty thousand Facebook servers). The server-side script on the server will access the database containing the user's information and generate the personal Facebook page that the user will see, transmitting it back to the user's browser.

In order to change the profile information, the user will hover over the Intro section below his profile picture and click on the pencil graphic. He then can edit or add to his profile. When he clicks on "update your information" and "save," the new profile is sent back to the Facebook database on the web server, and the scripting application updates the user information that is stored there.

Example Three: Doing Research

Websites that primarily provide informational content, like Wikipedia, have very simple scripting applications. If a user types in a search term on the Wikipedia website and clicks on the search button, the request is transmitted to the Wikipedia server. The scripting application finds the matching database and fills in the information it provides on an HTML template. The HTML file, containing all the database information, is then sent back to the user's browser.

Some informational websites, however, have more complex scripts. When a user requests the front page of a news site, the web server application may retrieve news stories from a database on the server combined with news stories retrieved from another website to generate a page that includes the most

Your Data Package Has Arrived

○ ○ ○

Programmers don't want to keep reinventing the wheel. They often look for a piece of reusable code that can be dropped into an application to perform frequently utilized functions, such as user authentication or database management. This reusable code is contained in libraries that programmers can access when they are looking for an efficient way to insert a certain function into the application they are writing.

Frequently, these libraries are collected together in groups called packages. The libraries in a package are either built upon each other or use each other in order to function most effectively. For example, library "A" may use code from library "D" in order to run effectively, so the programmer needs to download both "A" and "D" in order to run code "A." This relationship is called a dependency.

Managing dependencies can be a complex and sometimes messy problem, particularly if a project has multiple programmers calling upon a variety of packages to perform a variety of tasks. PHP Extension and Application Repository (PEAR) was an early system for distributing reusable PHP components. But PEAR was hard to search, hard to add new components to, and generally difficult to use, so many PHP programmers abandoned its use.

In 2012, Nils Adermann and Jordi Boggiano, two European developers, announced the release of Composer, a package dependency management tool for PHP. Unlike PEAR, Composer manages dependencies on a project-by-project basis rather than forcing a programmer to install packages on the entire system. It will download all the required libraries and packages and handle them in a meaningful and logical way. Its main package repository is "Packagist." Composer has now become an essential programming tool for most PHP projects.

Composer is a package dependency management tool.

current information. The page sent back to the client's browser may, in turn, be automatically updated by the web server application.

Example Four: Updating a Website

Websites built with server-side scripting, such as PHP, have some significant advantages when the user wants to update the site, particularly if the site consists of a large number of pages. If the website is created with a static code such as HTML, each page would have to be changed manually and uploaded when an update was needed. If, however, the site is created using PHP and MySQL as a linked database, the content could be updated for the entire site using the database. In order to update or alter the design, it would only require altering a small amount of PHP script.

How PHP Code Looks

PHP code can look very much like the HTML code that is used to produce web pages. Although PHP scripting can accomplish a great variety of tasks, it is deceptively simple to learn and use. At its most basic level, it can be embedded in an HTML page and simply create a static document, as though the code were completely HTML. All embedded PHP code is identified by beginning with <?php and ending with ?>.

For example:

```
<html>                              THIS SECTION IS HTML
<head>
<title> My first PHP script </title>
</head>
<body>
<?php                               EMBEDDED PHP CODE BEGINS
echo "Hello, Programmers!";
?>                                  EMBEDDED PHP CODE ENDS
</body>                             HTML CODE
</html>
```

This embedded PHP code will produce a static page with the message "Hello, Programmers!" This could also be achieved by using only HTML code. If, on the other hand, the code included a PHP variable, it would look like this:

```
<html>                              HTML CODE
<body>
<?php                               EMBEDDED PHP CODE
$txt1 = "Learn PHP";
$txt2 = "online";
echo $txt1 ";
echo "Study PHP $txt2";
?>
</body>                             HTML CODE
</html>
```

The output produced by this code would be:

Learn PHP
Study PHP online

Since this message is created using the variables identified as $txt1 and $txt2, the output can be changed by changing the variables. This is a step closer to a dynamic web page. If, however, the user fills out a form created in HTML and clicks the submit button, the PHP code that can process that request does much more. The PHP code will refer to the HTML code that created the form, as in the following example:

```
<html>                                HTML CODE
<body>

<form action="identity.php" method="post">
Name: <input type="text" name="name"><br>
E-mail: <input type="text" name="email"><br>
<input type="submit">
</form>

</body>
</html>
```

This HTML code will create a form for the user to complete that looks like this:

Name: [   ]

E-mail: [   ]

The user completes this form, clicks submit and the data is sent to a PHP file named “identity.php” so that it can be processed. The “identity.php” file (embedded in HTML) looks like this:

```
<html>                                HTML CODE
<body>

Welcome <?php echo $_POST["name"]; ?><br>          PHP
CODE BEGINS WITH <?php
```

```
The e-mail address you gave is: <?php echo $_
POST["email"]; ?>              PHP CODE ENDS WITH ?>

</body>                        HTML CODE
</html>
```

If the user's name was Harry and the email address entered was harry@mywebsite.com, the output on the user's computer would be:

> Welcome Harry
> The email address you gave is: harry@
> mywebsite.com

The PHP application on the web server took the data transmitted to it from the web form and generated a web page using that information. If the user was named Sally and her email was sally@mywebsite.com, the output would have been:

> Welcome Sally
> The email address you gave is: sally@
> mywebsite.com

This example is a simple demonstration of one of the ways in which PHP can personalize a user's web experience using simple code. More complex operations, including querying databases for information, validating input, and updating the databases, can all be accomplished with straightforward PHP code. PHP can do a lot with a little.

PHP

<Chapter Three/>

Strengths and Weaknesses

PHP was originally built simply to create web pages. Through the years of its continued evolution, it has maintained its focus as a web page development tool. Over time, though, it has matured into a powerful language whose immense popularity results from its significant benefits. The users of the huge number of websites that run on PHP experience these benefits, even if they don't all know that PHP is responsible.

PHP's popularity demonstrates the language's usefulness, but it doesn't necessarily mean that PHP does everything perfectly or that it never changes.

Opposite: Like any programming language, PHP has strengths and weaknesses.

software applications are run). This includes both open-source platforms and even the proprietary ones. PHP can function, for example, on Unix (its original platform), Linux, Windows, and mobile platforms such as iOS and Android. Some of its competitors, like JSP, also function on multiple platforms. Others, like ASP.NET, which functions only on Windows, are platform-dependent.

PHP also can also support a wide variety of web servers with different server software, including Apache (the world's most popular server), Microsoft **Internet Information Server (IIS)**, and a number of less standard servers, such as WAMPserver, and Oracle iPlanet. Then, too, PHP has cross-browser compatibility, working as well, for example, with Google Chrome as with Safari. Other scripting languages may, like ASP.NET, require additional scripting for browser compatibility.

Scott Guthrie is best known as the developer of ASP.NET.

It is also easy to find hosting service providers for PHP, while other languages, like Python, have operational requirements that can limit hosting options. PHP hosting can run under Windows (WAMP), Linux/

Unix (LAMP), Apple Mac (MAMP), Sun/Solaris (SAMP) and other web server software. ASP.NET runs under Windows, but in some cases for increased flexibility, it can use a virtual machine or **framework** in some other operating systems.

Server-side Scripting

One of the most important features of PHP is that it is a server-side application. This characteristic alone provides PHP with certain benefits. Unlike with client-side scripting, the user does not need to enable the scripts to run on their computer by downloading plug-ins, such as Java or Flash. With server-side scripting, the workload on the user's computer is reduced, because all the heavy lifting is being done on the server where the web page is actually being created.

PHP can also create those web pages "on the fly" based on user interactions, and the pages are often fairly quick to load. Using server-side **content management systems (CMS)**, like WordPress, website owners can create or maintain their own sites without the need to directly edit code. Users can also use external, readily available pre-written files (usually called libraries or packages) in order to save time and effort coding.

Then, too, the developer's scripts are hidden from the user, making the code more secure. Server-side scripting with PHP also protects the server from crashing. PHP runs in separate, isolated processes within the server software, and therefore it is very difficult for any single process to bring down the entire web server. When a request to the server is identified as a PHP file, the server gives that file to the PHP interpreter. The PHP interpreter then reads the file and executes the PHP code. When it is done, the PHP interpreter gives the output of the code back to the server. Since the PHP interpreter's state is totally reset at the beginning of each request, it is more reliable than systems with long-lived processes, and it ensures that errors will have a minimal effect.

On the other hand, with scripting software, all the necessary software and database(s) must be installed on the server in order for the scripts to function properly. In some cases, there are significant data security concerns because it is often easier for hackers to access servers where they can exploit flaws in the program code.

One researcher found that almost 78 percent of PHP applications were running with at least one known vulnerability. One of the most common weaknesses results from inadequate filtering of user input, allowing malicious code to be inserted into the application. Another frequent security problem is caused by SQL injections that occur when an attacker gains access to a database and subsequently to all of the website data. The most common security vulnerability, though, is known as cross-site scripting (XSS), which occurs when a hacker finds a way to get a visitor to a website to load pages with insecure coding, e.g., into a form inserted on a page that then transfers the user's input data to the hacker. All these vulnerabilities can be addressed by following best practices in PHP coding, but the popularity and ease of the language can often result in careless coding and increased security risks.

Simplicity

PHP was originally built using C, a general-purpose programming language. Because PHP's syntax remains similar, it is generally straightforward for C programmers to use. However, even for programmers without any knowledge of C, PHP has a quick learning curve, and it is fairly easy to become adept at coding in PHP.

Many programming languages are complex and require a complicated structural knowledge to accomplish tasks. A new PHP programmer, however, can learn a few basic functions and variables and begin coding. Another aspect that streamlines PHP is that it does not restrict documents to a specific order, and users adding new code don't have to make sure that that new code is in a specific place. Also, PHP does not need to be compiled before use since it is executed step-by-step during run-time, rather than turned into

ASP.NET and PHP

○ ○ ○

ASP.NET and PHP are both server-side scripting languages used in the development of dynamic web pages. Despite this essential similarity, however, they do have significant differences. One major distinction is cost. PHP is a free open-source tool, and ASP.NET is a Microsoft proprietary product. PHP runs on several platforms including Linux and Windows, while ASP.NET is designed for Windows implementation. Additionally, PHP can be run on a variety of servers, while ASP.NET is intended for an internet information server (IIS) created by Microsoft for use with Windows.

From a programming perspective, though, the ease with which PHP can be learned and implemented may provide the greatest contrast between the two languages. ASP.NET has a complex syntax and can be difficult to read and hard to learn. PHP, on the other hand, is so straightforward that novice programmers can often begin writing basic programs very quickly.

A comparison of the code to create a simple input form in these two languages clearly illustrates the differences.

The following is ASP.NET code:

```
<html>
<body>
@{
if (IsPost)
{
string name = Request["Name"];
string email = Request["Email"];
<p>You entered: <br>
```

```
Name: @name <br>
Email: @email </p>
}
else
{
<form method="post" action="">
Name:<br>
<input type="text" name="Name" value=""><br>
Email:<br><br>
<input type="text" name="Email" value=""><br><br>
<input type="submit" value="Submit" class="submit">
</form>
}
}
</body>
</html>
```

Alternatively, this PHP code can be implemented:

```
<html>
<body>

<form action="early.php" method="post">
Name: <input type="text" name="name"><br>
E-mail: <input type="text" name="email"><br>
<input type="submit">
</form>

</body>
</html>
```

In both instances, the output would be the following input form:

Name: [ ]

E-mail: [ ]

[Submit]

The differences in both the amount of code and its complexity are obvious. PHP can accomplish the same task with much greater simplicity.

machine-executable code in a separate step before it can be run.

PHP is not just suitable for novice coders without any other programming knowledge or experience, though. Developers who want to create more complex applications, can, for example, write custom extensions in C or C++ and will find well-defined and documented support for extending the functionality of PHP using this method. PHP is also easily and seamlessly embedded in other languages, most notably HTML.

The simplicity of PHP also makes it very easy to edit. PHP code is clear, and its purpose is easy to identify, so making changes is not complicated. Other languages require the user to change multiple functions within several documents in order to make the same changes that PHP can accomplish with limited changes in a single document.

Versatility

Although PHP is simple, it is also versatile. In addition to providing the freedom to choose any operating system and any web server, PHP is not limited to HTML output. PHP can output images, pdf files, Flash videos, and a variety of text files including XHTML and any other XML files. These files can be autogenerated by the PHP application and saved in the file system, forming a server-side **cache** for dynamic content.

PHP is as versatile as a Swiss army knife.

Although it's probably not the best use of PHP, it can even create desktop applications with a graphical user interface (GUI) in a client-side program. PHP can also extend its range through the use of command line scripting, making PHP run without any server or browser. These scripts can be used for some regularly scheduled tasks as well as simple text processing tasks.

PHP also supports many communication protocols including:

- Hypertext Transfer Protocol (HTTP), the foundation of data communication for the World Wide Web.
- Lightweight Directory Access Protocol (LDAP), a software protocol used to find individuals, organizations, and other resources within a network regardless

of if that network is public (on the internet), or private (on a corporate or organizational intranet).

- File Transfer Protocol (FTP), the standard protocol for transferring files from the server to the client.
- Internet Message Access Protocol (IMAP), a protocol for email that allows users to view and manipulate messages stored on a server as though they were stored on the user's own computer.
- Simple Network Management Protocol (SNMP), which collects information from network devices on an Internet Protocol (IP) network, such as servers, printers, hubs and routers, and configures those devices.
- Network News Transfer Protocol (NNTP), a protocol used to transmit news articles between news servers and posting articles in user applications.
- POP3, used to download email to the user from a mailbox on the server.
- Component Object Model (COM), Windows software that allows software components to communicate.
- Web Distributed Data eXchange (WDDX), that allows complex

data exchange between virtually all web-programming languages.

PHP also encompasses the two major conceptual models used in web programming. The procedural model is organized around functions that act on what are called data structures. On the other hand, object-oriented programming (OOP) uses objects, which incorporate both the data and the functions that act upon it. This flexibility allows PHP programmers to use procedural code for small projects where speed and coding ease are important. OOP allows for greater coding structure and better handling of complex and large-scale projects. The frameworks used in PHP applications are all designed with OOP and, although procedural coding may provide an easy entry into PHP programming, developers should be able to handle both methods.

Web Frameworks

Frameworks—standardized methods for building and organizing web applications—are a wonderful resource to help programmers build web programs more quickly and efficiently. PHP has a number of available frameworks that can make the programming process less complicated and time-consuming. These include Symfony, Laravel, CodeIgniter, CakePHP, and Zend Framework.

Content Management Systems

PHP also has a number of content management systems (CMS) that function to support web page management. Almost 60 percent of websites use content management systems. A CMS can, among other functions, allow a user to modify content on a website without being an administrator. CMS can also update websites quickly and easily.

Some of the many CMSs used with PHP include Composer, Drupal (written in PHP and has a community of more than 1.3 million members), Joomla (an open-source option), Magento, October CMS, and WordPress. WordPress is identified as a blog tool, publishing platform, and CMS; it's used by more than 25 percent of the world's websites.

Performance

PHP developers have worked diligently to improve its performance. More recent developments seem to have helped PHP speed up significantly. With PHP 7.0, "on the fly" optimizations have been incorporated. Facebook has created an open-source runtime engine—originally called the HipHop Virtual Machine, now just HHVM—that is said to execute PHP commands almost six times faster than the standard PHP interpreter. HHVM now powers Facebook, and other large PHP users are adopting it as well.

Database Support

One of the most powerful strengths of PHP is its support for a wide array of databases. A PHP application can access databases in a variety of ways: using a database specific extension, such as MySQLi; using PHP Data Objects (PDO) to connect to database drivers other than MySQL; or using other methodologies like cURL. And the number of PHP-supported databases is enormous, and includes, among others, Access, Adabas D, dBase, Ingres, InterBase, Empress, Oracle FrontBase, FilePro, PostgreSQL, Sybase, mSQL, Solid, Hyperwave, DB2, Velocis, Informix, ODBC, and Unix dbm.

MySQL is the database most frequently used with PHP applications, and the code can interface with it and integrate the strength of the database and its relational organization into the PHP application. This ability also reduces the development time for web applications.

Libraries

Since PHP is very popular, it has a large community of developers that contribute by crafting PHP components that help other programmers build their own projects more easily. These components are stored and accessed through PHP libraries. Since the resources are so extensive, however, finding the right components requires organization and support.

Repositories

Software repositories are web-hosting facilities that contain file archives for a large amount of source code. They provide storage from which software can be accessed and installed. They often provide additional services that may include **version control** (logical management and identification of software changes), release management (controlling a software development through different stages), and bug tracking (a database providing information about a software package's known bugs), as well as documentation. Some repositories for PHP code include PEAR, FSD, SourceForge, GitHub, and Packagist.

Library Examples

Writing PHP code can be monotonous, repetitive, and time-consuming. Many of the features that make PHP sites appealing and functional do not necessarily require code that is uniquely designed for a particular application; they can be implemented using code written by other developers and are available to download using PHP libraries. Libraries contain pre-written code that can provide a variety of functionality, save coding time, and allow developers to focus on other aspects of web design.

If a developer wants to enhance the images on a website, for example, Image Workshop is an open-

Access is a commonly used relational database from Microsoft.

source library that allows image manipulation such as cropping, resizing, and creating watermarks and thumbnails. Snappy, another PHP library, supports snapshot, pdf, or thumbnail generation from an HTML page.

Assistance with PHP and MySQL development is provided by PHP DB Class, a library that reduces the amount of coding required to access a database. PHP DB Class also provides a variety of debugging features. If a developer wants to create a tree hierarchy from a database, Tree is another library that can make that easy.

PHPMailer is an essential PHP library backed by a huge community and implemented in popular

MySQL and PHP

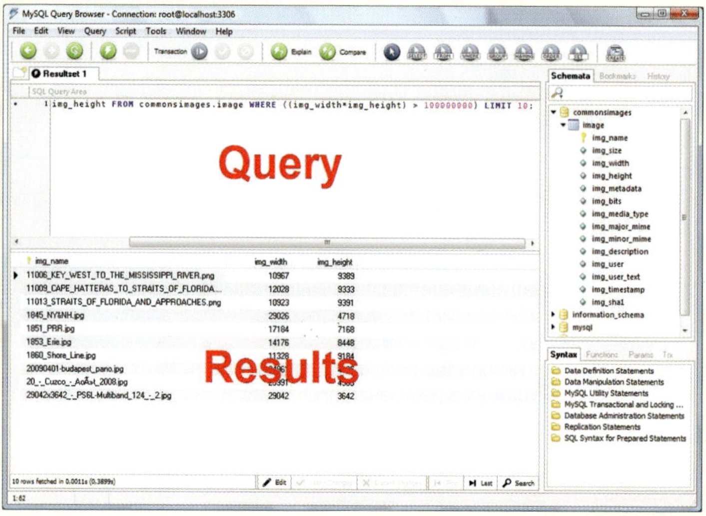

MySQL is the most frequently used database for web-based applications.

MySQL is an open-source database that has become the most popular data management tool to use for web-based applications. MySQL is the database of choice that handles information for many well-known sites including Facebook, Twitter, YouTube, and Wikipedia. It not only stores information, but it allows users to manipulate and access the data it holds in a variety of ways, through what is known as a **structured query language (SQL)**. Like PHP, MySQL information is stored on the server, and it performs all its tasks there. Since one of the most powerful ways in which PHP functions is through working with databases, effective use of PHP requires understanding and implementation of databases like MySQL.

The data in MySQL is stored in collections of related data entries placed in columns and rows called tables. In order to use the MySQL database in a PHP application, the database must first be created and connected. A table for accepting the input data must be created. The following code provides an example of this process, containing both PHP instructions and MySQL code.

```
<?php
$servername = "localhost";
$username = "username";
$password = "password";
$dbname = "DB1";

/*The PHP application must be connected to MySQL
-The extension used is actually MySQLi, the improved
version of MySQL - and the successful execution of that
connection should be checked, using, for example, the
following code:*/

$conn = mysqli_connect($servername, $username,
$password, $database1);
if (!$conn) {
   die("Connection failed: " . mysqli_connect_error());
}
echo "Connected successfully";

/*A table that contains the data that will be used in the
PHP application is then created in the MySQL database,
using MySQL instruction*/

$sql = "CREATE TABLE MyCustomers (
id INT(6) UNSIGNED AUTO_INCREMENT PRIMARY KEY,
firstname VARCHAR(30) NOT NULL,
lastname VARCHAR(30) NOT NULL,
email VARCHAR(50),

)";

if (mysqli_query($conn, $sql)) {
   echo "Table MyCustomers created successfully";
} else {
   echo "Error creating table: " . mysqli_error($conn);
}

mysqli_close($conn);
?>
```

MySQL and PHP (continued)

○ ○ ○

The PHP program can perform a number of operations using the databases created in MySQL. Using a customer database as an example, among other functions, it can:

- Insert new data into the database based on user input. Every time a new customer places an order, a new customer record can be added to the current database.
- Update the data on an existing database, changing billing information or shipping address based on new user information.
- Retrieve information from a database to provide current information to a user, such as the status of an order.
- Delete records from a database if, for example, a customer choses to eliminate a previously used credit card.
- Perform logical and arithmetic operations on the information in the database, calculating, for example, the sales tax on a customer's purchase.

When the data has been extracted from the MySQL database, the PHP application generates a web page in HTML that is transferred back to the client browser and displayed for the user. As just one example of its power, PHP, combined with MySQL, can make online purchasing a seemingly seamless event.

Michael Widenius created MySQL.

systems such as WordPress and Drupal. Developers often chose it as the safest library to use for sending emails in PHP. It has SMTP support and can do HTML-based emails. Swift Mailer, another email library, sends emails quickly and efficiently from PHP websites with minimized pressure on server resources.

Business projects can be created more easily using a number of libraries such as PHP Excel, phpDocumentor, and Pchart. PHP Excel allows developers to implement applications that include spreadsheet editing. The library called phpDocumentor supports the creation and automation of professional documents using PHP code. It incorporates many features to assist in the generation of customized documents including tutorials and documentation linking and cross-referencing through highlighted source code. One called pChart can assist in the generation of a visual presentation of text data. It can create charts, graphs, and more, using SQL queries.

When a developer has a problem with an application, Whoops is a library that helps with PHP debugging and displays a detailed error listing. It provides the specific files and code snippets that caused the problem with highlighted syntax. Though the number of PHP libraries and extensions is enormous, understanding the wide range of functions they can perform can save a lot of coding time.

<Chapter Four/>

Getting Started

Because PHP is so widely used and has such amazing capabilities, learning the language can open up a lot of possibilities. Maybe you want to use PHP as you build a personal website. Maybe you are thinking about pursuing a career in computer programming. Either way, learning PHP is a worthy goal and one that can be accomplished by programmers of all skill levels.

PHP Employment Opportunities

Programming with PHP is a very popular activity. Virtually every survey of software developers and

Opposite: Getting an early start with PHP can help you secure a great job.

College courses in computer science cover much more than a single programming language.

additional subjects such as computer architecture, object-oriented programming, and operating systems, as well as essential coding skills. They may, in addition, require courses in advanced mathematics.

Learning PHP coding may not be included in the basic coursework necessary to get a degree, but it is often provided as an optional course. Many developers will seek internships while still in school to acquire important on-the-job experience. The foundations provided by an academic education, however, can provide the footing not only for high-level work in the computer sciences. They can also provide the fundamentals that make it easier for a programmer to decide on the appropriate language for a particular task, understand the best design choices, and follow the best logic and practices for creating clean and refined code.

PHP Training

The popularity of the language has resulted in many opportunities for learning PHP in ways tailored to fit all preferences, including nonacademic. Google executives have noted that "the proportion of people without any college education at Google has increased over time," and being a successful PHP developer does not actually require any degree.

Among the alternative options for learning PHP are online courses. There are a great variety of structured online PHP courses. Some have live online instructors,

Coding boot camps are a popular option and can help attendees become fluent in a language in a short period of time.

like Udemy, or provide a certification, like the Zend Technologies PHP courses. PHP 101 provides a lighthearted program for absolute beginners. Others like Killer PHP offer video instruction, and, in addition to PHP, videos in other related topics, such as object-oriented programming and MySQL.

Another option is PHP boot camp. These schools often pledge to turn you into an employable developer upon completion of their program. They usually require three to four months of full-time attendance, although some offer part-time or online intensives. Most of the time in a boot camp is spent building projects, rather than listening to lectures, so the graduates finish with products that can be used to demonstrate the skills they have acquired.

According to Matt Mullenweg, creator of WordPress, making contributions to the open-source technology community "[gets] you to the top of the list when we're reviewing applications."

Those who don't want to enroll in a program, or even follow a structured set of videos, have many opportunities for learning PHP that are both accessible and convenient as self-taught learners. Rasmus Lerdorf, the originator of PHP, suggests:

> Just dive in and download some code. Start solving problems using PHP. I often joke that

> I can teach a moderately intelligent monkey to write PHP in a day. The learning curve is really shallow, so you'll get up and running really fast.

Some have found Lerdorf's rather tongue-in-cheek advice to ring true as far as learning the specific coding details of PHP by doing, since the language itself is so clear and simple. The background and foundations necessary to create elegant and effective applications using PHP, though, requires more than basic coding skills. Yet, for those who have an understanding of the conventions and structures of general purpose programming, acquiring PHP coding skills can be accomplished relatively quickly.

One of the most useful resources for this method of learning the language is the PHP manual at php.net. The manual contains the source code of the most recent versions of PHP as well as contributions by members of the PHP community and the answers to FAQs. This immersion in the PHP community not only helps with PHP skills, it can build networking that supports becoming a PHP programmer.

"Citizen Developers"

One of the movements in the technological community is the rise of the "citizen developer." These are not professional programmers, but rather amateurs who

Matt Mullenweg

In 2003, Matt Mullenweg and his friend Matt Little started WordPress, the open-source web software built primarily using PHP. As of 2017, WordPress is the most popular content management software and is used by noted websites such as USA Today, CNN, Fortune, Time, and NBC. Seventeen blog posts are published to WordPress sites every second, and fifty thousand WordPress.com websites are being launched each day. Amazingly, this software powerhouse was started by Mullenweg when he was a nineteen-year-old freshman at the University of Houston.

As a teenager, while studying music at Houston's High School for the Performing and Visual Arts, Mullenweg began building websites for local jazz musicians, combining his love of both music and technology. Then, during Mullenweg's brief attendance at the University of Houston, he met Matt Little online, discussing a blogging tool they were both trying to improve. WordPress was born. By the following year, WordPress was beginning to take off, and Mullenweg was offered a job in San Francisco with CNET, working for them on WordPress and other media initiatives. Although his parents were concerned about Mullenweg leaving college, they were supportive, and Mullenweg accepted the offer.

Matt Mullenweg started WordPress at nineteen.

PHP was the primary language used to build WordPress.

After one year at CNET, Mullenweg went out on his own to concentrate on WordPress full time. He founded Automattic, which continues as the WordPress software development company. He has been an acknowledged technology innovator from the beginning. Mullenweg was named one of the fifty most important people on the web by *PC World*, received Temple University's Information Technology Award, was identified as one of the Top 30 Entrepreneurs under 30 by *Inc.* magazine, and named one of the 25 Most Influential People on the Web by *BusinessWeek*. His awards and acknowledgements continue to recognize his accomplishments.

Mullenweg identified the approach to innovation that helped him create WordPress:

> The vast majority of what impacts our whole life is taking something and making it better or taking two things that didn't work together before and putting them together, like

Matt Mullenweg (continued)

○ ○ ○

> peanut butter and chocolate. I was taking many things that were out there before like open-source, publishing, blogging, everything, and putting them together … It requires incredible dedication and perseverance and hard work and elbow grease to [make] innovations actually matter in the world. Otherwise, it's just an idea, and ideas are a dime a dozen.

While continuing to work as CEO of Automattic, Mullenweg also began supporting start-ups through his advising investment company, Audrey Capital. He has become involved in numerous philanthropic activities, including the Apache Foundation, which supports open-source products for the public good; charity:water,which helps to bring clean water around the world to those in need; and the Electronic Frontier Foundation, which defends human rights in the digital world.

Despite his multitude of activities, Mullenweg revisited his early passion for hands-on technology and announced in 2017 that he was returning to "leading core WordPress development for several releases," as WordPress incorporated more JavaScript into its front-end interface, while preserving back-end PHP technologies. He describes this new effort:

> I'll say as well that learning new things is scary. Personally, I now have thirteen years' experience coding in PHP, and you kind of have to—if you're learning a new language—you're kind of back in that beginner phase which can be frustrating at first … But PHP is still really fantastic for server-side stuff.

use programming tools to build applications within their corporate environments. Companies are always looking for new applications to address business issues, and IT departments can't always meet the demand, particularly for products like mobile apps. So, citizen developers, who have learned programmer skills but whose job titles don't identify them as developers, have filled the gap.

Many of these citizen developers have no formal computer science or software engineering degree. They identified a need in their business and decided to address it. The rewards for these initiatives have been notable. Many, according to a survey by FileMaker, report more organizational recognition and greater confidence and higher work satisfaction, and 71 percent report an increase in team productivity. Citizen developers prove that you don't need to have a job as a developer to make meaningful contributions as a programmer.

Getting Ahead

PHP is the most-used language in web development, and its implementation is simple and straightforward. But on its own, it does not always provide a full set of tools for developing a complex and dynamic web presence. PHP programmers have greater power and flexibility when they can incorporate certain concepts in their work, use other languages that facilitate PHP development, and employ other structures, such as frameworks, that can make their programming both easier and better.

Procedural Programming and OOPs

Developers may use two different approaches when figuring out how to solve a programming problem. These approaches are **procedural programming** and OOP, and both are supported with PHP. Most early programming languages, like COBOL and C, are procedural languages. In this technique, the focus is on the processing. The programmer creates a set of procedures (functions) that act upon data, e.g., "a" gets added to "b" to produce "c." Functions (like adding) and the data that is being acted upon (for example,

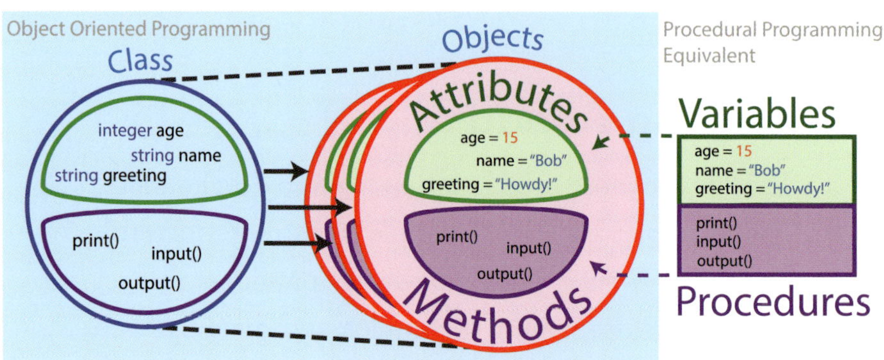

This graphic shows how object-oriented programming (OOP) and procedural programming name the same elements.

a product cost and shipping cost) are separated from each other.

On the other hand, object-oriented programming was first implemented in the 1960s to provide graphically oriented applications for simulations. It became more popular in the 1970s with the creation of C++, an OOP version of the C language. OOP places the object (e.g., singer) and its attributes (e.g., song) together in a single structure. Objects know how to perform certain actions (for example, sing) and how to interact with other elements of the program (for example, lyrics and instruments).

There have been long-standing debates about the relative merits of the two different methods. Proponents of procedural programming maintain that it is capable of high performance and can provide quick design and implementation. OOP adherents, on the other hand, point out that large projects and collaborative efforts are easier with OOP. Maintaining and modifying existing code as new objects can be accomplished with small changes to existing ones.

Since both have their advantages and disadvantages, a PHP developer who can choose the appropriate method for a given project will be able to create applications that can function better in the present and adapt to necessary changes in the future.

Critical Languages

PHP works best when it is implemented with other languages that add to its functionality, including markup, style sheet, data, and programming languages. The most essential of these are HTML, Cascading Style Sheets (CSS), MySQL, and JavaScript.

HTML, first developed by Tim Berners-Lee in 1990, is known as the basic building block of the World Wide Web. It creates documents on the web and describes how those documents are structured. There are not many components to HTML and its format is simple. For example:

```
<!doctype html>
<html>
<head>
<title>Example of HTML</title>
</head>
<body>
<h1> This is a heading example</h1>
<p> This is a basic HTML page example</p>
</body>
</html>
```

These markup instructions create a basic web page using tags that identify the different elements of the page such as headings and paragraphs. The browser uses HTML to specify the structure and content of the web page. HTML can be written on any text editor including an HTML editor. PHP applications creating dynamic web pages are embedded in the HTML that creates the basic static page.

Tim Berners-Lee developed HTML in 1990. He is also the inventor of the World Wide Web.

Although the HTML code is essential, it is also limited. It does not usually specify the way the information on the web page should look. For that, CSS is necessary.

CSS is a structured language that describes the presentation of a web page. It is a basic technology used by most web developers to create the look of web pages and user interfaces for web and mobile applications. Its development created an alternative to the exhaustive HTML instructions needed to specify such elements as font colors, background styles, paragraph alignments, borders, and sizes. CSS, through separating formatting from content, can control how HTML content is displayed on computer screens, paper, and other media.

web page does not have to be reloaded and refreshed with every update. For the user, web surfing can be an uninterrupted experience while the content is still continuously updated.

JavaScript can facilitate catchy animations and even simple calculations. Its code can provide **event handling**, reacting to things that occur in the browser. This can range from user actions like resizing the window or scrolling the page to using information in a link to connect to a web server. It can pass user values to the server and accept values transmitted back to the browser.

Web developers use PHP and JavaScript as complementary tools with different purposes, using both client-side scripting and server-side scripting to create a web experience that is both highly responsive and highly engaging.

Other Languages Worth Knowing

Although web development is usually executed with specific languages intended for that purpose, a knowledge of general-purpose programming languages increases a developer's skill and flexibility, as well as providing the ability to tackle larger, more sophisticated projects. Many websites depend for their implementation on these general-purpose languages, like Java and C.

Java is a general-purpose language that was designed to be platform-independent. A Java Virtual Machine, which interprets Java binary code for a computer's hardware, exists for most operating systems. It can run Java code after its processing by a **compiler**. Java is an object-oriented language similar to C++ but with less complex coding. It is a very popular language for web development and, according to Oracle, Java's owner, there are more than nine million Java developers. Java is on more than three million mobile phones.

Java has a number of features that make it well adapted for use as a web programming language, but applications will not work unless Java is installed on the browser. It is particularly popular with high traffic websites because Java is able to outdo other languages in speed and reliability. Java is used, for example on high-volume sites such as Amazon, Sam's Club, LinkedIn, Netflix, and the Apple App Store. It's also the programming language used to develop all native Android apps (the apps that come loaded on Android devices).

Scripting languages, such as PHP, can be connected with a Java Virtual Machine through the PHP/Java Bridge, promoting much speedier and reliable performance and using fewer web server resources. It requires no additional components in order to call Java procedures from PHP or PHP procedures from Java.

C is also a general-purpose programming language. Its constructs closely represent the functions of machine instructions, so it has been used in highly technical applications from operating systems to supercomputers. It was originally developed between 1969 and 1973, and many later languages have borrowed recognizable expressions and syntax from C, including C++, Java, JavaScript, C#, and Python. Rasmus Lerdorf, creator of the original implementation of PHP, coded it in C.

C can also be used for website programming, using CGI (a common gateway interface) as a way to pass information between the browser, the server, and the web application. It may be selected for its speed, ability, and easy availability. But, although C is the foundation of many web-development languages and tools, most developers see its complexity and time-intensive coding as major drawbacks that keep it from being really useful in creating websites.

What's in the Future

The changes happening in technology are explosive. And the World Wide Web, with what we can learn from it and what we can do with it, is at the center of this change. PHP is striving to stay not just relevant, but instrumental in fostering new developments. Some of these developments include the expansion of mobile apps, artificial intelligence, and the Internet of Things (IoT).

The Expansion of Mobile Applications

Cell phones have become so familiar and ubiquitous, it is sometimes difficult to realize that they are a relatively recent and still-developing technology. The market for mobile apps on these devices can seem endless, and new apps are continuously being created.

The overwhelming majority of PHP developers are working on, or plan to work on, mobile apps. The process of implementing mobile apps with PHP is still being refined and continues to present some challenges. Marrying the web technology with the mobile device architecture can be difficult. But the

Mobile apps can do almost anything. Many PHP developers work on mobile apps as their core work.

advantages of PHP coding—less typing, safety and simplicity, and first-class functions—make it very appealing to mobile developers.

The support for developing PHP mobile apps is also expanding, and there are new frameworks for providing this assistance. Zend On The Go is a sample mobile application that shows how to create mobile apps using existing PHP applications. It monitors the new application and gives server performance statistics. Zend Studio helps developers create a cloud-connected mobile (CCM) project using PHP back-end functions. GitHub, an enormous version control repository, contains an ever-growing collection of supports for mobile app development using PHP.

Artificial Intelligence (AI)

Artificial intelligence attempts to understand how intelligent entities (like humans) function and build intelligent entities (such as robots) that have those attributes. This complex and challenging field is producing new ideas and innovations, and PHP development is right there in the mix.

An artificial neural network (ANN) is a computational model built to simulate the way people think. An ANN is composed of neurons that communicate and provide output. Although it is still very primitive, an ANN can be used for prediction, classification, and decision-support systems, as well as applications. ANNs have primarily been developed in high-level languages such as C or C++, but PHP has been found to be the most convenient way to implement AI in web applications, so it has been used to create neural networks.

Artificial Linguistic Internet Computer Entity (A.L.I.C.E.) is a bot (internet robot) that is capable of holding a conversation and responding with relevant answers to questions. A.L.I.C.E. responds to the Artificial Intelligence Markup Language (AIML), which is used to give the bot instructions on how to "think." Implementation of this bot in PHP is called Program E.

AI bots may be used for informational communication, such as Siri or the iPhone bot. A number of PHP forums on AIML provide PHP users with information and support for the development of AI applications.

IoT

The Internet of Things (IoT) allows devices on a network to sense and collect information from other connected devices, process that data, and use it for a variety of purposes. Ordinary household appliances and devices can be connected with IoT to perform a wondrous range of tasks. For example:

- Your watch can track your daily activities and exercise and match it to goals you are working to attain.
- A wearable device can monitor your blood pressure and notify a health care professional of your status and possible need for care.
- A motion-detecting camera can notify you if an intruder is on your property.

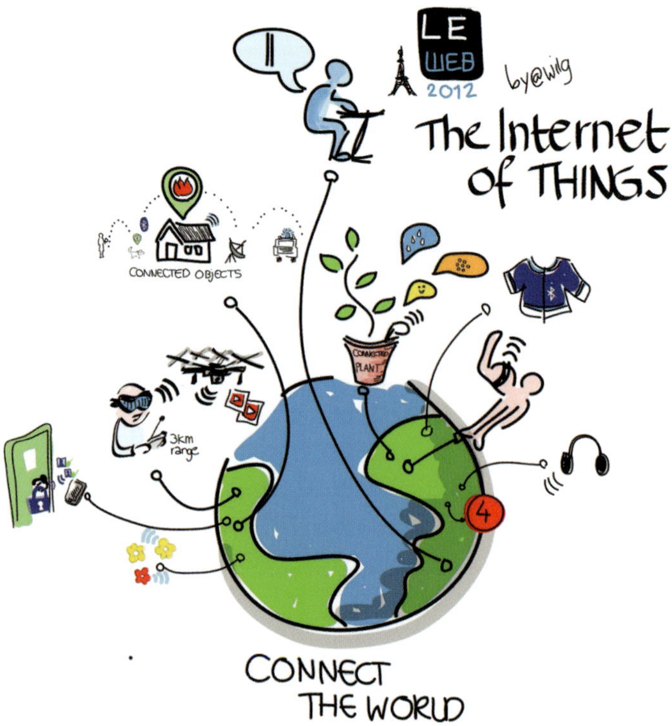

The Internet of Things is a network of smart devices.

- Your refrigerator can order groceries when your supplies are low.
- Your heating system can notify the oil company when you need a delivery.

The list of possible applications can go on and on, and IoT provides great opportunities for PHP developers. PHP is an ideal language for IoT applications. Its flexibility and affordability foretell a great future for PHP programs in the IoT world, creating almost any connection the developer can envision.

PHP: A Language in Motion

PHP began as a simple tool for coding a personal home page and has evolved over time into one of the most popular languages for creating dynamic websites. Now it is moving into applications that will serve future technology. Throughout its history, it has continued, as it began, by responding to old problems, and by changing as it solved new problems. It has been criticized for slow performance, but it keeps adding speed. It has been called limited and basic, yet it keeps adding new features to increase its power and sophistication. It started with web pages and is now growing into artificial intelligence.

PHP has countered its critics through the strength of a dedicated and enthusiastic community that provides ongoing support for resolving any difficulties and creates extensive documentation for every new attribute. Its popularity has been linked to how easy it is to learn, but its endurance stems more from its ability to modify and transform itself into the right solution for the time.

<Glossary/>

application A type of software that allows you to perform specific tasks.

Application Program Interface (API) An interface that specifies how software components should interact.

asynchronicity Communication (as between computers) in which there is no timing requirement for transmission.

cache Reserved areas of computer memory that are used to speed up instruction execution, data retrieval, and data updating.

common gateway interface (CGI) An interface that provides a standard way for a web server to pass a user's request to an application program and to receive data back.

compiler A software program that transforms high-level source code into machine language, which can be understood by the processor.

content management system (CMS) A computer application that supports the creation and modification of digital content.

cookies Small text files that allow the server to store its information about a user on the user's own computer.

CPU The central processing unit of a computer where calculations are carried out.

developer A programmer who specializes in the creating of World Wide Web applications.

DOM The document object model, which is used for changing the elements of an HTML document.

engine A program that performs a core or essential function for other programs.

event handling Processing actions such as keystrokes and mouse movements.

eXtensible Markup Language (XML) A language designed to store and transport data.

framework For PHP programs, frameworks specify programming interfaces, or offer programming tools for using the frameworks.

HTML A language that describes and defines the content of a web page.

HTTP A protocol that defines how messages are formatted and transmitted on the World Wide Web and what actions web servers and browsers should take in response to various commands.

Internet Information Server (IIS) A flexible, general-purpose Microsoft web server that runs on Windows systems.

interpreter A computer program that executes instructions written in a programming language.

JIT compiler A program that turns Java bytecode (a program that contains instructions that must be interpreted) into instructions that can be sent directly to the processor.

module A software component or part of a program that contains one or more routines.

object-oriented programming (OOP)
A programming language model organized around objects rather than procedural actions, and data rather than logic.

open-source Software for which the original source code is made freely available and may be redistributed and modified.

operator A symbol that represents a specific action, e.g., a plus sign (+) is an operator that represents addition.

parser A compiler or interpreter component that breaks data into smaller elements for easy translation into another language.

procedural programming A computing method that uses a series of steps to be carried out.

proprietary software A technology or product that is owned exclusively by a single company.

protocols Sets of rules governing the exchange or transmission of data between devices.

relational database management system (RDBMS)
A database management system that lets you create, update, and administer a relational database.

scripting language A programming language capable of many tasks, including generating web pages on the internet.

semantics The evaluation of the meaning of characters, words, and symbols in a specific programming language.

server A computer or computer program that manages access to a centralized resource or service in a network.

software stack A group of programs that work in tandem to produce a result or achieve a common goal.

structured query language (SQL) A language used in programming and designed for managing data held in a relational database management system.

syntax Grammatical structure.

Unix A family of multitasking, multiuser computer operating systems.

version control The management of changes to documents, computer programs, large websites, and other collections of information.

web form An online page that allows for user input.

<Further Information/>

Books

Forbes, Alan. *The Joy of PHP: A Beginner's Guide to Programming Interactive Web Applications with PHP and MySQL*. Rowley, MA: Plum Island Publishing, 2015.

Lengstorf, Jason, and Thomas Blom Hansen. *PHP for Absolute Beginners.* New York: Apress, 2014.

Lockhart, Josh. *Modern PHP: New Features and Good Practices.* Sebastopol, CA: O'Reilly Media, 2015.

Ullman, Larry. *PHP and MySQL for Dynamic Web Sites: Visual QuickPro Guide* (4th Edition). San Francisco: Peachpit Press, 2011.

Websites

Object-Oriented Programming

https://www.cs.drexel.edu/~introcs/Fa15/notes/06.1_OOP/titleslide.html?CurrentSlide=0

Learn more about OOP on this site from Drexel University.

PHP

http://php.net/

The official website for the PHP community includes information about new releases, documentation, and more.

PHP the Right Way

http://www.phptherightway.com/

Explore this resource for new PHP programmers.

Videos

PHP Tutorial 1 – Introduction (PHP for Beginners)

https://www.youtube.com/watch?v=kY5P9sZqFas

Watch the first in a set of twenty-five PHP tutorial videos followed by four MySQL videos.

The Ultimate Guide for Learning HTML and CSS

https://www.youtube.com/watch?v=y3UH2gAhwPI

Learn how to make websites from scratch.

<Bibliography/>

Hassan, Anita. "WordPress Founder Finds Inspiration in His Hometown of Houston," *Chron*, September 28, 2016. http://www.chron.com/local/history/innovators-inventions/article/Wordpress-founder-finds-inspiration-in-his-9403035.php#photo-11118668.

Hulme, George, "Meet the Citizen Developer." *Devops*, February 3, 2017. https://devops.com/meet-citizen-developer/.

Kingston Central School System Alumni Association. "Rasmus Lerdorf." Retrieved March 14, 2017. static1.1.sqspcdn.com/static/f/1560920/20510047/1349287039360/Rasmus+Lerdorf.pdf?token=GokG2XTT%2B47LGWBNFk1oEvULQFM%3D.

Krill, Paul. "Believe the hype: PHP founder backs Facebook's HipHop technology." *Infoworld*, November 13, 2013. http://www.infoworld.com/article/2609877/web-development/believe-the-hype--php-founder-backs-facebook-s-hiphop-technology.html.

MIT. "Technology Review: Innovators under 35 – 2003." Retrieved March 14, 2017. http://www2.technologyreview.com/tr35/profile.aspx?trid=347.

MySQL Conference. "PHP on Hormones." April 26, 2007. http://talks.php.net/show/mysql07key/.

O'Dell, J. "Why this web guru wants you to learn PHP, a.k.a. 'Internet English.'" *Venture Beat*, September 21, 2012. https://venturebeat.com/2012/09/21/treehouse-php/.

U.S. News and World Report. "U.S. News and World Report Announces the 2017 Best Jobs." January 11, 2017. http://money.usnews.com//money/careers/articles/how-us-news-ranks-the-best-jobs.

Wayner, Peter. "9 predictions for the future of programming." *Infoworld*, January 18, 2016. http://www.infoworld.com/article/3022874/application-development/9-predictions-for-the-future-of-programming.html.

Wodehouse, Carey. "PHP: The Language, Its Frameworks, and How to Hire the Right PHP Developer." *Upworks*. Retrieved April 1, 2017. https://www.upwork.com/hiring/development/php-frameworks-hiring-a-php-developer/.

Zmievski, Andrei. "The Good, the Bad, and the Ugly: What Happened to Unicode and PHP." *In Slideshare*, April 22, 2011. http://www.slideshare.net/andreizm/the-good-the-bad-and-the-ugly-what-happened-to-unicode-and-php-6.

<Index/>

Page numbers in **boldface** are illustrations. Entries in **boldface** are glossary terms.

<Index/>

<About the Author/>

Grace Murphy has authored books, white papers, speeches, encyclopedia articles, and online courses in history, economics, and science. Grace has also worked as an educational consultant, health care administrator, computer programmer, and college teacher. Grace is the author of *Semiconductors* in the Great Discoveries in Science series. She currently lives in the peaceful hamlet of Shady, New York, where she enjoys regular hikes on the local mountain trails.